How to Start a Landscapir

RIGHT NOW! With NO Star

Keith Kalfas

The Landscaping Employee Trap

Get the AudioBook Version Too

On Amazon and Audible or @

www.TheLandscapingEmployeeTrap.com

How to Start a Landscaping Business

RIGHT NOW! With NO Startup Money

Introduction

Are you sick and tired of working in a dead-end job for someone else? aka
being someone else's bitch!
Sick of barely making enough to pay the bills? aka broke-ass
Sick of fighting with your significant other over money?
Sick of running your ass off like a slave for peanuts?
Sick of being bitched at for having to use the bathroom?
I could go on and on and on.

But...
You want to start your own damn landscaping company!
But...
Don't have the money to get started.
But...
You Don't know how to get started.
But...
You're terrified of failing and losing everything?

But...
Your spouse is attacking you and everyone around you is either stupid...
negative... or holding you back..
But... But... But...

See?
This book is just for you Brother...Read on...

Chapter 1

THE VICTIM AT WORK

The time was 6:53am...

I was driving to work to my dead-end landscape job.
I had tears of frustration rolling down my cheeks and bags under my eyes.
I punched the steering wheel in my car so hard that I almost broke it.
I was sick and tired of being sick and tired. Day after day, week after week,

month after month.
I thought my hard work would pay off. I thought leaving the last company

and walking into this one as a foreman would have made a difference by
now. I thought the slightly higher pay and added responsibility would finally
get me noticed.

That "one day I'll be the high-paid guy who gets paid to drive around
in the truck all day" delusion had me caught up in a total lie.

There's a saying that goes, "look at someone who's been doing what
you're doing 5 years longer than you have and that's probably where
you'll be in 5 years".

All these thoughts were churning through my head that summer morning. It
was only 6:55am at this point and already the sun was blazing through the
windshield of my 99' Intrepid.

I looked in the rear-view mirror into my own eyes, I didn't fucking even
recognize myself anymore.

Being forced out onto my own at 14 years of age, sleeping on couches until
18 then having to pay for an apartment etc. at such a young age.
I practically fell into landscaping, helping my old man cut lawns in his own
small lawn care business at the age of 11.
Then lying about my age on a job application through a newspaper ad at
17.
So on the story went, going from company to company. 3 years here,
2 years there. It was a love hate relationship.
I loved the freedom of cutting grass, working outside, listening to my ipod
all day, but no matter what the circumstance, I was always near-broke, or
broke.

By this time it was 6:58 and start time was 7:00a.m and I had pulled into
the employee parking lot of the very large company I was currently

enslaved, oops I mean employed to.

Now I want to make a distinction between enslaved and employed.
I damn well knew It was my choice as a man as well as every man's choice
to punch a clock every day.

I'm also aware that the company appreciated my presence.
After all, I loved my job, I took pride in being on time every day.
Being in the top 10% of the highest skilled guys in the industry,
running crews and banging out jobs with meticulous attention to
detail.

Landscaping is in my blood and I really felt like an important player in that
company.
Plus I learned invaluable skills and technologies by the leaders in that
company that I didn't know would help change my life one day.
It's the slave part that gets me.

A lot of times I did feel like a slave, it was even part of my vocabulary.
"Slaving for the man", "Slaving in the sun all day".
Hell yes I felt like a slave! But why? We'll let me ask YOU.

Chapter 2

ARE YOU A SLAVE

Do you feel like a slave? Do you feel trapped? Do you really think a bullshit
raise is really going to change anything in your life?

Let me enlighten you on the things that took me years to understand.
There's a saying by Tony Robbins. "Change happens in an instant, but
sometimes it can take years to get to that point".
You see, what I'm referring here to is the "victim mindset". The mindset of a 2 year old, crying in front of the gumball machine at the
grocery store.

So what is a victim?
A victim is a person who's convinced themselves that their not at fault for
where they ended up in their own lives.
That circumstance is to blame. Their childhood, their socio-economic
status, aka (broke ass family).

Their father or mother died when they were young. They have imagined
mental or depression problems.

(I'm not talking about the true unfortunate with real health or mental
problems).

I'm talking about the true victim-minded excusers that put everyone else
and the world around them to either blame or cry out as the reason why
they're stuck in a current situation that they "Claim" they don't want to be in.
You get my point here? That was me.
That was me all day and to tell you the truth. It wasn't that noticeable,

I did a GREAT job of concealing my own faults and victim-mindedness to myself and others through "Self-Deception".
Self-deception is amazing because it covers it's own tracks.
We're not even aware that we're doing it.

Chapter 3

Start Becoming Aware

So to get on with the story. I basically felt like a slave because I didn't
know how to get out, I was trapped in a system of thinking that was imposed
upon me by other people since birth.

Day after day of grueling in the hot sun I would bring these topics up to my
co-workers.
I would ask. What the fuck are we doing here?
We make just just barely enough loot to pay our bills, then we show up
Monday and do it all over again.

"How do we get like these rich people were landscaping for? How did
the owner of this huge company get started? I heard he started many
years ago with a push mower."

On and on I would ask questions and be rejected as if I thought I was better
than everyone else. On and on I would sneak my ipod into work and listen
to dozens of personal-development programs on audiobook while working.
But my newfound wisdom always fell on deaf ears. I even once was
threatened to be

fired from the company if I didn't shape up and start acting like everyone
else.
I started realizing that I was playing in a losing game. That the tables were
tilted and that nobody, not even the managers had a real chance at not
only financial independence, but independence at all.

During these dark times, I thought about every possible way out.
From the old "I'm going back to school", to " I'm going to find a better job",
to every other bullshit excuse in the book.
Layer upon layer, like a jawbreaker I was filled with self-doubt and reasons
why I was doomed to work for another man all because I didn't have the
startup capital or $10,000 to start my own damn company.

Besides, In truth, I didn't even want to start my own company.
I was too busy spending my nights and weekends doing live music shows
trying to become the next famous solo-artist. But that's a whole other story
for a whole other time.

After watching all my former landscaping bosses pull their hair out trying to
run their own businesses.
All the nightmare stories of sue-happy employees, pissed off, non-paying

customers and all the rumor hearsay crap "from non-business owners" of
how risky starting your own business is and how many businesses fail.
I was trapped.

Or at least I believed I was.

Chapter 4

THE GATEKEEPER

The Gatekeeper is what's keeping you from setting your sails.
The Gatekeeper is the mysticism you believe that's holding you back.
The Gatekeeper is the bullshit stories you keep telling yourself.
The Gatekeeper is the feelings of unworthiness you're suffering from
The Gatekeeper is other people's opinions about what's possible
The Gatekeeper is...

YOU! YOU! YOU!
YOU! Are the Gatekeeper

YOU! Are the only one who can take responsibility for your own life.
YOU! Are not a child anymore and it's time to dissolve your inner child.

THE INNER EWW

There's a saying I once heard that makes a lot of sense.
it goes.

"You know how you know when you're totally done with a relationship?
it's when the very thought of that person gives you an inner eww."
That feeling of disgust.

Have you had that feeling of disgust in yourself?
Napoleon Hill in his hit book "Think and Grow Rich" said "You have to develop and alter ego, then live into that new person"
Go look in the mirror and get disgusted with yourself.
Decide today to no longer be a slave to your own fear.
False
Evidence
Appearing
Real

Chapter 5

ABOUT FEAR

Attention: This chapter is very important, so don't be lazy and skip over
it.
It has everything to do with getting your new landscaping business off the
ground.

Fear plays the major role you're resisting the development of new habits.
Fear is what's really stopping you from stepping out into the unknown and
launching your new business.

AND...

Fear is really nothing more than an unconscious part of your brain
responsible for firing off signals to protect you from annihilation and death.
Wikipedia says:"Fear is an emotion induced by a threat perceived by
living entities, which causes a change in brain and organ function and
ultimately a change in behavior, such as running away, hiding or freezing
from traumatic events.

Fear may occur in response to a specific stimulus happening in the

present, or to a future situation, which is perceived as risk to health or life,
status, power, security, or in the case of humans wealth or anything held
valuable.

The fear response arises from the perception of danger leading to
confrontation with or escape from/avoiding the threat (also known as the
fight-or-flight response), which in extreme cases of fear (horror and terror)
can be a freeze response or paralysis."

Let's talk about fight or flight.
There's 3 different parts of our brain that have developed or (evolved)
over the past several million year.
These 3 parts are known as the "TRIUNE BRAIN" or the New Brain.

They're responsible
1.) the "old brain" or Reptilian brain stem. (Responsible for fight or
flight) hence: Eat, Sleep, Get Laid.. Survive... lol

2.) The "recent brain" or Mammalian Brain
(Responsible for Nurturing) hence: Emotions, parenting, living in
community, bla, bla, bla.

3.) The "new brain" or Neocortex (Responsible for Higher Evolvement)

Hence: Planning, Perceptions, Organizing and basically all the intelligent
shit humans can do...

Compared to the the rest of the animal kingdom,,
So...
That being said.

There's a part of the brain called the "Amygdala"
keep reading...
This part of your brain keeps you BROKE and in FEAR!

It's what causes you to go into anxiety and not be able to face your
problems...
It's what makes you make stupid short term decisions...
The smallest thing like an unexpected flat tire or bill in the mail can trigger
this thing to put you into a panic state and lose access to all resources.

When this thing gets triggered by an external stimuli, "FEAR" it literally
shuts off the conscious and logically intelligent areas of the brain.
And...
You become a chimpanzee temporarily, or even worse...
A reptile....And no, I'm not talking about Reptilians...
I mean you literally lose consciousness and turn into a higher primate that
has no option in those moments but to STAY ALIVE.
Here's the CATCH...

Chapter 6

YOUR BRAINS NOT WIRED FOR BUSINESS

Your Brain is Wired to keep you alive.
(NOT getting a landscaping business off the ground.)
Your brain comes wired from the factory to keep you safe, secure and to
do "WHAT THE HELL EVERYONE ELSE DOES"
how .."THEY ALWAYS DONE IT".
It basically keeps you from getting eaten.

So...If you're used to working at a job with a weekly paycheck.
Doing something that you might not get paid for right away,
or just plain not knowing if your going to get paid at all, can give you some
serious anxiety.

Like, you don't know how to price out and quote jobs yet.
Do you know how much to charge?
How much extra to charge per man hr. for employees?
how much to charge for materials, mulch, topsoil?
Where to find suppliers, how to get it delivered, where to dump?
On and on...the very uncertainty of not knowing the next thing to do.

"The fear of the unknown" can put you into serious
"fight or flight MODE" It can literally FEEL like you're dying.
Especially if you're Broke and can't afford ANY mistakes.
I've been there and that's why I'm writing this book for you.
That's why I started the Landscaping Employee Trap.

I know what it's like to be flat broke, to suffer and run around in constant
anxiety.

I've been homeless, lived on people's couches, failed miserably..
bla bla bla...
WHAT'S THE POINT OF FEAR
The point is...when you begin to understand the way the brain works,
you can start objectifying your fears.

You can start to see that Fear is inside of everyone...

Especially me..

Not too much about myself, but more to help you.
Ill tell you that I live in almost constant fear and anxiety.
I have nightmares and panic attacks, obsessing about my life falling apart,
getting sued, losing everything, my wife leaving me because she ultimately
decides I'm crazy and she can't handle my obsession with success
anymore and blee blee bla..

Shit bro..I'm getting anxiety even typing about this stuff right now.. haha.
But trust me dude. I'm not lying to you when I tell you...That I'm nowhere
near perfect.

Don't be watching my YouTube channel and think I'm some kind of

smart businessman. Because most everything I learned, I learned it all
from reading audio books and watching Youtube videos.

I chose to better myself instead of hanging out with my friends and fucking
around. NOT because I want to sit around and read books all day, but
because I'm TERRIFIED and in FEAR of where my life will end up if I don't.
See, That's the point of fear.

People will do more to avoid the shit they DON'T want to happen instead of
the shit they DO want to happen.

Chapter 7

WHAT YOU DON'T WANT

Here's the WHY question.

If you've watched my videos then you definitely know that I talk about
having a WHY.
Yes... but I'm not asking you what you want in life.
I'm asking you what you DON'T want.
Yes.. What the hell do you NOT want to happen in your life?

Who's lifestyle around you can you think of that scares the living daylights
out of you? Someone in your family? A close friend? A group of friends?
There's a saying I like, it goes.
"take a look at a thing your doing, then also take a look at someone
who's been doing that thing 5 years longer than you have, and... that's
probably where you'll be in 5 years."
Man, life is passing you by at the speed of a ticking clock.
How long are you going to wait to change and get this thing done?

When the pain of dealing with what you DON'T want get's so bad.. that
changing is actually less painful than staying the same... you'll change.
WHAT DO YOU WANT?
Now we're talking. See, it all comes down to the WHY.

When y0u can figure out your WHY in life and figure out what you WANT.
Figuring out how to get there isn't so bad anymore.
It doesn't matter how hard you try to get something accomplished.
If you don't know why you're doing it than you won't have the tenacity to push
yourself through the tough times.
Especially when getting a small business off the ground.

What do you want in your life? Time with family?
To be able to afford a nice home? All the bills paid, food in the fridge?
To be able to take care of an ill or old grandparent? etc.

Think of a time when something sad happened in your family life and no

one had the time or money to solve that problem.
What if it could've been you that solved it? What if there were no
Christmas presents under the tree growing up in your house?
I'm just giving some of my own examples here, but I really want you to
think hard about your life and figure out not only what you WANT, but
WHY you want that stuff and what WILL happen if you don't make that

stuff happen.
See... I'm trying to get you locked in from both angles here.

which brings me to my next point.

Chapter 8

MOTIVATION

I love the old Tony Robbins talk about

"Fear and incentive motivation."
He says,.."There's two types of Motivation, Fear motivation and incentive
motivation", "What your running to and what you're running from", "and both
WORK"
Cuz I'll tell you man, 80% of the success in my life has all come from FEAR
motivation. The pain and suffering of have low self-esteem and being
flat-ass broke all the time was too much for me.

SOOOOO PAINFUL, when you look around and see people laughing and
smiling and shit, but you're all pissed off thinking about your cell phone bill,
ya know what I'm saying man?

MAN UP...MAN

So man up, Man.... Pound on your chest and start visualizing yourself living
the life you want to live. Even if it takes getting mad and flipping out and
breaking shit.

You gotta change, you deserve it bro. You deserve the best life has to
offer. Screw the naysayers, these fools opinions don't control you.
You are the creator of your destiny and getting a landscaping or lawn care
business off the ground is eezy-greezy shit man.
Compared to running an insurance company, a Legal office, You Name it.
This is EZ Street.
It's Like playing in the sand-box. Its seriously NO WHERE near as hard as
continuing to be broke as fuck and not living your dreams.

Nuff Said!

TAKE THE RISK

"It's time to leave pookie and them, back at the sandbox".It's time to take a calculated risk.
Yes it's scary, but what other options do you really have?
Were you born
with a silver spoon in your mouth?
Does mommy and daddy have a big family business that your being
groomed to take over?
Yea, Probably not. Nothing is going to change until you take the risk and
change it. If you want to have your own badass landscaping company, then

take the risk. Starting out with 1 weekly lawn care account isn't going to
make your deepest fears come true. It's going to excite you.
Screw the "too risky" folks, because having a job is too risky,

"Risky is the new safe".

Chapter 9

LET'S GET YOUR BUSINESS OFF THE GROUND

OK...So you're already plenty Motivated and ready to get on the ball and get
your lawn care & Landscaping Business off the ground.

All these principles apply to almost every small business by the way too.
There's a saying I once heard. it goes. "Methods are many, Principles are
few. Methods always change, Principles never do".
These are fundamental business principles that never change.

A Zen student once turned to his wise master while sitting by a stream and
asked. "Master... What is Real?"The master turned to him and answered...
"That which never changes"...

Ok enough with the philosophy. I've brainwashed myself with so many
damn books over the last 10 years I could vomit.
So.. let's get the plane off the ground baby...

GETTING THE PLANE OFF THE GROUND

When a plane is taking off from the runway, it needs full throttle, peddle to
the metal. No slowing down, because even if at the last couple seconds... if

the pilot throttles down. "like a little bitch"

The PLANE AIN'T GOIN NOWHERE...
You have to fully decide that come hell or high water, this is where the buck
stops. and it's with you. Now that you've decided 100%
That no amount of rejection is going to stop you, it is only going to be fuel
for your success.

Cuz I'll tell you right now. I may be going on and on and you're like "Keith..get
to the nuts and bolts already. But I'm telling you. All the nuts and bolts in
the world aren't going to prepare anymore than a driving reason why and a
hell bent determination that your going to WIN at this.

Chapter 10

MARKETING

If you don't know jack about marketing, well now is the time to learn.
Marketing is what makes the phone ring.
Marketing is How you communicate to the world that you're in business.
Marketing (Just like Money) is the OXYGEN of your business.
You have to start marketing your business for visibility purposes, because
the more visible you are... the more the phone rings.. the more quotes you
book... the more jobs you sell... the more jobs you complete... the more
money you make. Marketing is you standing on your soapbox and
repeatedly yell..."HEY EVERYONE... I'M IN BUSINESS.

NAMING YOUR BUSINESS

To me... this is obvious...Name your business something cool, or you last
name or something.(Not giving legal advice here)

Example: Joe Blows Lawn & Landscape. tadaa..
Don't name it something stupid.. lol

METHODS OF MARKETING

Below is a list of all the (NO cost to HIGH cost) ways you can use to market your business. We also calls these "Lead Sources"

YOUR MARKETING TOOLBOX

TANGIBLE DIY (Low-Cost)

1. Business Cards

2. Door Hangers

3. Flyers

4. Postcards

5. Brochures

6. Magnets

7. Stickers

8. Pens

9. Coffee Mugs

10. Bandit Signs

INTERNET (No-Cost)

1. Craigslist Ads

2. YP.com

3. Angies List

4. Yelp

5. Google Places for Business

6. Bing

7. Yahoo

8. YellowBot

9. Yahoo

10. MapQuest

11. Your Website

SOCIAL MEDIA (No-Cost)

1. Facebook Business Page

2. Twitter

3. Linkedin

4. Pinterest

5. Instagram

6. YouTube

7. Myspace.

8. Vine

9. Google+

PRINTED MEDIA (Medium-Cost)

1. Newspaper

2. Magazines

3. Trade Magazines

4. Direct Mailings

5. Coupons

6. Save-On Magazines

7. Community Mailers

8. Coffee Shop Digests

BROADCAST MEDIA (High-Cost)

1. Radio

2. Television

3. Cable TV

DON'T SPEND MONEY ON MARKETING

At first....
No Lies...My crazy obsession with finding NO-Cost or LOW-Cost ways to
market my Landscaping business has really paid off for me in a big way.
Why? Because I was flipping BROKE as a JOKE! I didn't have a dollar to

spare so ..I found an amazing book that I recommend called "Guerilla
Marketing" by Jay Conrad Levinson. It's all about Low Cost or No

COST ways to market your business.

This book had me running around like a mad man putting wire bandit signs
in the Michigan turnarounds of busy intersections, passing out business
cards, approaching total strangers, and building social media profiles until
my eyes bled. What I'm saying is you can totally market your business for
close to free in the beginning.
Speaking of free...Want to get the phone ringing right now?

Chapter 11

THE POWER OF CRAIGSLIST

Thank you Craig! Wow. I've built my entire business off of Craigslist ads.
Even some of my best friends I've met off Craigslist.
Yes Man! If you want to get your business rolling fast. Create like 4 email
addresses and then create 4 Craigslist accounts.
Then Start posting your ass off. Refer to my video On YouTube

(The Landscaping Employee Trap "12 Craigslist Ads a Day")

Start out by taking the digital image of your business card and using as the
main pic in your posting. Then either take pictures of your real work or steal
them from Google images. Pictures of Lawns being cut, Sunny skies yada
yada.

Anything to make your business look legit. So a Sample Craigslist Ads
looks Like this.

DISCLAIMER: This is basic beginners marketing copy and serves a basic

purpose. We're not going to get into marketing psychology and
high-persuasion selling techniques.

So... thru the eyes of Top Marketing Experts like Dan Kennedy.
This Ad is Lame and non-enticing.
Learning how to post million dollar ads...Comes in time.
Below is an example to get the ball rolling.

Subject Line:

Joe Blows Lawn Care & Landscaping

or Lawns Cut $20 for (YOUR CITY)

or Lawn Care Maintenance (Best Deals in Town)

Content: ...

Joe Blows Lawn Care & Landscaping

Where integrity comes first

1(888)555-1212

Proudly Serving the (YOUR CITY) area

- Lawn Care

- Shrub Trimming

- Landscaping

- Garden Bed Maintenance

Ask about our Deals on Mulch installations This month

Call 1(888)555-1212

Joe Blow - Owner

MAYBE:

A short company bio.. like....

established in 2014, Joe Blow company took a shit in the woods

an accidently found a push mower, just kidding...

Joe Blow Company est 2014 has been preserving and beautifying

properties in (YOUR CITY). Joe Blow Company guarantees results to

its clients and is licensed insured-highly referred.

Now unless this looks professional, don't try it...

But if you can pull it off, the older people love this stuff and it will give them

an instant sense of trust.

Yours Truly...Mo Money...

REMEMBER

Nobody cares about you, they care about themselves.
Once they meet you and you make their property look fantastic.
Like 4 or 5 times in a row...
Then, they'll start to care about YOU. lol

Trust me bro, I've made all these mistakes X10.
If I could only show you how stupid my first 3 months of ads were.
And some of the dumb as shit I said to customers, I'd go jump off a bridge
in shame.

There's a saying I'm reminded of taught by my wise Uncle Ed.
It goes..."People don't care how much you know, until they know how much
you care".
Keep repeating that in your head every-time you post an ad or communicate with your clients or prospects in any way, shape or form.

TADAA!

Simple shit right? Take that and its varying combinations and throw some
catchy pictures in there and now you've got yourself a Craigslist Ad son.
DO NOT! Put personal information or how good of work you do, or how you
feel or any of that stupid shit. That will make people NOT call you and you
will stay broke. Less is more. Your ad should communicate STRUCTURE

and professionalism. People should feel a sense of trust and authority
when they read your ad. You can add a small company bio or mission
statement at the bottom if you chose. But make it about the company and
not about YOU.

NOW...Go and Create at least 3 different Craigslist ads and START
POSTING...and Keep making more and more ads until you have about 20
of them. I personally have 6 CL accounts and over 80 different ads that I
post CONSTANTLY. I post 3 in the morning, 3 at lunch, 3 @ 4pm and 3
more in the evening.

When your always posting... you're always at the top of the list and
your phone will ring that much more. Sometimes you can post all day
long and no one will call. Sometimes you'll post just an ad or 2 and
the phone will ring off the hook.
Nevermind, just keep posting and make it a daily habit.

I literally start posting ads in the morning while sitting in the toilet.
Posting while letting my dog out. Posting while making coffee, and so on.

Chapter 12

INTERNET MARKETING

NUTS & BOLTS

OR.. The basics of SEO. Everyone is talking about SEO, That's a gigantic
relevant subject. Too much for this book, But I'll tell you.
Go to Audible.com and buy the book called SEO Black Book.
It will change your life.

I'm not going to bore you to death with SEO stuff here because it's a
constantly evolving plethora of controversy. But when it comes to marketing
your landscaping business online I'll tell you this. Get online in every free
way, shape or form possible.

Once you get your basic graphic design, company logo and short bio going.
Run to the arena of the internet and start building social profiles. Here's an
example.

BUILD PROFILES

Go to every single website online that will allow you to build a company
profile for free and do it ASAP.
This is very similar to these companies that call your phone all day and try

to sell you #1 spots on Google. If these companies and telemarketers
aren't calling you off the hook all damn day then you're in for a real treat.
Once your company starts developing an internet presence, they'll be
bugging the heck out of you.

Some of them are reputable companies like YO, Yext, Yelp and Home
Advisor are great but they all cost Money. That's not going to make
any sense for you right now if you don't have any fucking money yet.
So, get on

Facebook business

YP.com

Yelp

Angies List

Yellowbot

Google+

Yahoo Business

Myspace

Instagram

Twitter

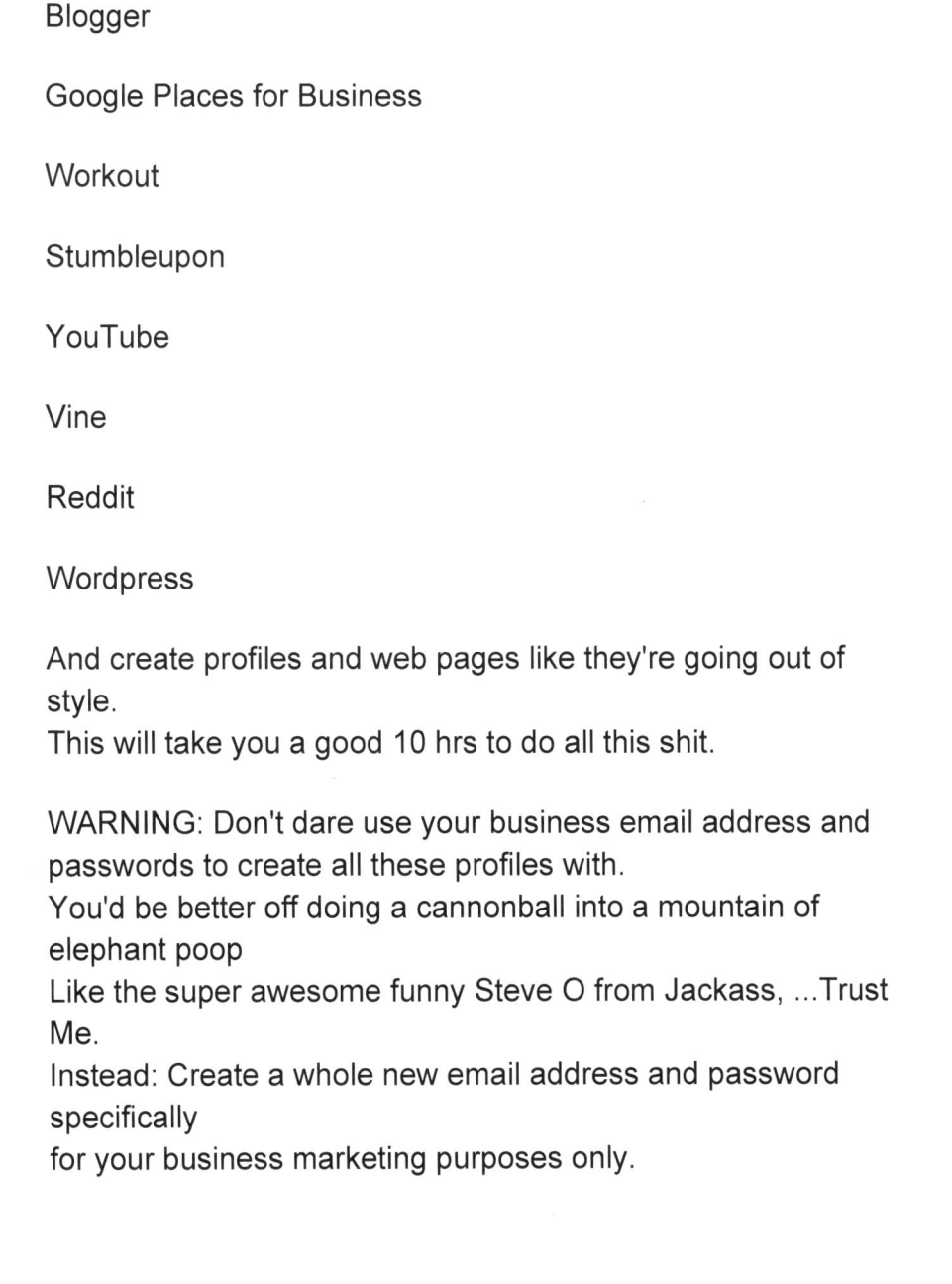

Pinterest

Livejournal

Blogger

Google Places for Business

Workout

Stumbleupon

YouTube

Vine

Reddit

Wordpress

And create profiles and web pages like they're going out of style.
This will take you a good 10 hrs to do all this shit.

WARNING: Don't dare use your business email address and passwords to create all these profiles with.
You'd be better off doing a cannonball into a mountain of elephant poop
Like the super awesome funny Steve O from Jackass, ...Trust Me.
Instead: Create a whole new email address and password specifically
for your business marketing purposes only.

MARKETING ONLINE CONTINUED

Pay Attention, Shit's Gettin Deep
But once you have all these profiles built, all with a short company
biographies, pics , graphics and all that jazz. (Just like making 20 new

Facebook pages, but on 20 different websites)

Now Open up a notepad and copy/paste your new unique URL addresses
of every single new website profile you've launched
and title every URL to match the name of your website.

Here's some URL examples below,

Facebook

http://www.facebook.com/thelandscapingemployeetrap

Twitter

http://www.twitter.com/theemployeetrap

YouTube

http://www.YouTube.com/themployeetrap

Website

http://www.TheLandscapingEmployeeTrap

The "Http://" Thing is code for "Go here" or "Clickable link".

Once you build an entire notepad on your computer of all these url's
combined with your company bio. Now you can begin to start building your
own "backlinks" or "create an inter-connecting spider-web" of internet
connections that allow your landscaping business to more easily be found
online.

SIDE NOTE:

"For instance if someone finds you on Google+ or Yahoo.
They'll be able to see the links the other links to your website and
Facebook Business Page RIGHT THEN RIGHT THERE and... They'll be
able to click on it and be taken instantly, to your website or FB page
etc.

and... if they happen to be on your FB page... there will be links to
your Google+ and all your other stuff right there too."
"See? Backlinks is Uber important and the more you have the merrier.
That's partly how people blow up online, by having tons of content all linked
to other content. But more-so by having other people sharing your content
as well."

Continued...

So "highlight and copy" the entire contents of your notepad, with all 5,7 0r
10 of the new profile URL's you've created in one bunch.
Now go back into the social media profiles you created one by one and
paste the URL's into the bio section of those profiles.
For example, the about me section of your Facebook profile.
Paste all those flipping URLs inside of there.
Get it? So now people can track your business down on the internet easier
and faster. Some profiles like Google+ have personal programmable
URL's link options in the "Edit your BIO" settings.
So now you can paste all of those URL's in there and start creating your
empire online.

I really hope you're getting this. It's like throwing mud at the wall of the internet. Google takes up to an entire year to "INDEX" your website. That means, Google doesn't give a crap if your website has been online

since 1809'. It only starts giving credit the day it "INDEXes" it. Which means "Credible". So start building your website, social media and
business profiles right away, everywhere you can, RIGHT NOW.

Next, go on all those Profiles and start sharing relevant content.
Which means. Write a couple sentences about Lawn care on your

Facebook page, and share that shit to your Google+ Page. Then take the stuff on your Google+ page and share that stuff on your Yelp
bio.

Then take your Yelp Page.... and share that URL' to your Facebook
page. on and on. A red-headed step-child could do this. Once you get the ball rolling, it's like a ferris-wheel. you get the point,

I've drilled deep enough for this section.

Just go do it!

Chapter 13

5 STAR REVIEWS

Here we go Freaks!

And no I'm not copying Geek to Freak. Geek to Freak is his own badass
with his own empire of freakiness. lol
So welcome to 5 star reviews. This is important stuff man.

When you get your Yelp, Angies List. Facebook Business, Google
Business etc. Profiles set up. It's important to get 5 star reviews as soon as
possible. When people go online and look up your company.

"Social Proof" Plays a huge role. You can start out by having your friends,
family members and customers leave 5 star reviews on your sites. In the
future you can even take screenshots of those reviews and post them on
your website.

In the far out future you can get audio recordings of 5 star reviews, video
testimonials, on and.

REFERRALS

Referrals are the heartbeat of your business. You'll soon learn that in the beginning. There ain't no referrals, because ain't no-one knows about your

bitch-ass.
So you're gonna have to rely on Craigslist, Newspapers bla bla bla.
But once you get the ball rolling and start priming the pump. Referrals are
like icing on the cake. They're the lowest cost cost - to highest profit ratio
thing that can happen inside your landscaping business.
There's a badass book I read a couple times on audio-book called "The
Referral Engine" by John Jantsch.
You can purchase it on Audible.com. Read that book. He has several
other great books too about business systems.

Referrals are 70%-80% of my entire business now. Once customers

like you and get comfortable with you, they want to refer you to their
friends and family as well. So keep your Clients close, take care of
them and never let them down. Even the crappy customers have led
me into entire networks of high profile clientele.

So the power of referrals is where most of the money is going to flow into
your landscaping business.

B2B Referrals - Commercial Work

People always want to know how to get commercial work. Here's a huge
way it works, when you become a business owner. You start attracting
other business owners as friends and clients into your life.

Let's say you cut Johnny Dillhole's lawn for 6 months and make friends with
him. Soon you learn that he runs a huge commercial shop in the middle of
town and they're annual contract is up for grabs.
If you got your act together and Johnny Dillhole like your bitch-ass. Then
who the fuck do you think he's gonna think of? Sure ain't the milk-man. It's You!

Business Cards

I hope you get a chance to see some of my YouTube videos about carrying
business cards with you everywhere you go.
I'm a firm believer that what you think about expands. So, carrying
business cards around in your pocket or even a little clip on cell phone
pouch puts you in a powerful position to win.

PASS THEM OUT LIKE CRAZY. You can design them yourself on Paint,

Microsoft Word, Photoshop, etc. or go to Fiverr.com, Elance.com,
Odesk.com and hire a freelancer to design them..

Or hire a local graphic designer off Craigslist or your local print shop will
provide designs for you.
Business cards are the #1 first item you NEED above all else.
If you want them printed online. I use VistaPrint.com, UPrinting.com

Door Hangers & Flyers

Door Hangers & Flyers work the best during springtime and busy season,
but they do work all year long. Once you get a couple bucks together... hit
those subdivisions like a madman.
Also hit up the SAME subdivisions several times over the period of a
month. They don't have to look perfect. Just clear and to the point.
Refer to Craigslist ads section of this book.

Chapter 14

AMAZING STORY

I have an AMAZING Story to tell you about How magical getting a business
off the ground is and only those bold enough to fly out on their own will ever
have the precious privilege to experience this.
It's the law of POSITIVE EXPECTANCY!

My first year in business I was flat broke and on the phone trying to place a
local newspaper ad.
It was $24.00. But I remembered that I didn't have my bank card on me.
Just as I was about to cancel the ad, my wife pulled out her bank card and
handed it to me. I placed a tiny, cheap ad.
A week went by, the ad came out, no calls. 2 weeks went by no calls.
Dammit. Waste of money. At the end of 2 weeks, a little old lady called me
and asked for a quote. I went there and was disappointed because she had
like 12 teeny-tiny little shrubs and the price came out to like $27 or
$37dollars.

So I booked the job. I figured at least I could introduce myself to the
neighbors and pass out business cards
around the neighborhood.

Remember I was flat broke and hustling to survive. I had just quit my
jobs only days earlier and was running on a shoestring to get this
business off the ground.

Whaddya know, while trimming that old lady's shrubs, the next door
neighbor comes outside and asks me for a quote. Yes I said..
It came out
to $280 bucks to trim all her shrubs on her property.
I sold the job on the spot and booked it.
The very next day while doing that job. The original old lady comes out and
happily tells me that her "son in law down the street" would like an estimate
as well.

I immediately got his contact info, called him up in front of her and booked

the quote. Directly after finishing the lady's shrubs and collecting the $280
and dripping in sweat from head to toe.
(I booked her again for the fall trimming).
Then hopped in my rusted out truck and ran right over to the Son in law
guys house and sold him a $800 Landscaping project. BOOYA!
I booked the landscape project and finished it within a couple days.

Here where it gets good...

While banging out that guys landscape project at his newly purchased
house. His old man was working in the garage and noticed how hard I was
working. He mentioned to me that his
other son was a real-estate investor and needed some help sprucing up a
couple properties that were getting ready to hit the market.

I instantly gave the old man a couple business cards and insisted that he
have the investor call me. That very same day the guy called me and I
dropped everything I was doing and went straight over to the property.
"I left an entire job site a total mess in the pouring rain, exhausted,
almost flat broke and starving to death"

When I arrived at the property the owner was there waiting.
We walked the property and even though I was intimidated at the size of
the project, I was also stunned at the fact that it was really just a bunch of
small projects all bundled up into one large project.

"I've done Gigantic fucking projects with crews of guys when I worked at
big companies... and we had all the tools necessary.
But now being on my own with some minor hand-tools and a shitty pickup
truck, was a real slap in the face."

The guy was impressed that I knew every plant, exactly what to do, how
much mulch and so on. he was more impressed with my cheap prices. So
I sold the job on the spot for $1,400. BOOM!
Booked it for the following week and banged it out.

Here's Where it gets Even Better...
While doing the big landscape job, he calls me up and says that now he
has ANOTHER house down the street he wants taken care of.

I sold and booked that one... BAM! Then the guys aunt calls me and
wants HER property trimmed... BANG! Then the flippin neighbor came
outside from across the street and I sold her a $600 job on the spot that
took only 4hrs. KAZAAM! then sold that customer an $1,800 project where I
made $1,000 in ONE DAY.. ALAKAZAM BITCHES!

See where I'm going here? Ya See?

Do I have to jump out of this book and slap you in the face? lol.
It's The LAW of POSITIVE EXPECTANCY at work here baby!
It's the 8th wonder of the world.
Excited Yet? Can you Imagine those Dollaz Yet?

Chapter 15

WORD OF MOUTH

If there's one thing people do well, It's talk, talk, talk. Word of mouth will
explode your business. hopefully it's good words too.
there's a saying and don't forget it. "People will talk about 10% of what you
do right and 90% of what you do wrong".

Word of mouth is the best form of advertising so always remember.
The most powerful thing I ever learned in network marketing.
"One person represents one-hundred people".
Ok, What the hell does that mean right? It literally means that one person,
on average, knows around one-hundred people.

So keep a tight ship because even if you get stuck servicing annoying or
cheap customer, that one customer could be the gateway to 99 more
customers. All through the power of the word of mouth.

THE POWER OF THE TONGUE

So just a reminder about all this word of mouth stuff. I'm serious here. I
care about your success and I want you to succeed at his.
Now that you own your own Landscaping company, you gotta start
monitoring everything you say.

I'm not referring to your best buddies here, I am referring to everyone
else including Your cool Client Billy Bob Who You Think Because
You've been mowing his lawn for 6 months now is your friend.
He might be your friend, But he's NOT.. I repeat He is NOT.. your best
buddy.

What I mean here is. Everything you say either puts money in your pocket
or takes money away.
Whenever you sit at the counter in a restaurant or bar. What do you say
during small-talk with the people around you? What do you say amongst
groups of strangers? behind closed doors? On the phone?

How do you think and talk about people?
The tongue is like a sword and can cut like a razor brother.
You'd be surprised how small the world is and how many people know
everyone else... and you didn't even know it. People talk.

What are people saying about you behind your back? Do they say your a
backstabber? A greedy shit talker? A rip off? A Liar?

I'll talk more about this later, but being in business is all about Integrity.
So...If people only have good things to say about you when you're not

present. Then Good Word of mouth referrals will flow into your life. Jobs will
seem to come out of nowhere at just the right time when you needed them
most, or least expected them.

That's how powerful your, and others tongues are...the power to
MAKE OR BREAK Your Landscaping Business.

Chapter 16

Selling and Booking Jobs

This reminds me of some of my favorite books. They are "must reads".

#1 The Magic of thinking Big

#2 How I raised myself from failure to success in selling

#3 How to win friends and influence people

That's enough for now. But Selling isn't really selling like you think it is.
The classic high-pressure salesman or furniture guy thing doesn't work
anymore. Nothing against car salesman, it's just a Cliche'.

But True selling is more about being present and available for your
customer. Talk very little and just listen to them. Be a professional,

NEVER let the conversation go in a negative direction. Always pretend you were being videotaped. Haha. True selling is not
about SELLING them on more work. I've learned that Traditional selling
just backfires. True Selling is being in the spirit of service while maintaining
a strong backbone.

When booking jobs it can be as simple as a verbal agreement and
hand-shake, all the way to signing contracts with down-payments and proof
of general liability insurance.

Not going into contracts here, but you can download and use free invoice
templates inside Microsoft Word. You write a description of work being
performed, both of each-other's contact information, sign and date and
walaa!

The more of your own information you have in print.. the faster and easier
the process goes. Just get a simple work order printed up then go make

copies... as you grow your business, you'll find more things that need to be

on the work order.
Every few months, go back and revise the work order so it's more
professional each time, then print more. walaa!
When you actually book the jobs, I prefer the Google calendar.
(I have a YouTube video about it) The Google calendar is amazing
because BOOM.. it's digital, cloud based and allows you to schedule an
entire business right inside your smart phone.
Yes it's going to suck at first, but train yourself to start using a digital

calendar until it becomes habit and you'll never be late or miss an
appointment ever again.

Chapter 17

ACQUIRING EQUIPMENT

I have a Video on YouTube called "How to Start a Landscaping Company,
Even if you're FLAT BROKE".
You gotta see it, I literally break the process down step by step.
What I mean here is. You don't need thousands of dollars to get
equipment. I started out with all used stuff from Craigslist, pawnshops,
garage sales, my uncles garage etc.
Shit man, I remember pulling up to this garage sale my second summer in
business and walking out with over a $1,000 in hand tools, shovels, wheel
barrows, sledge hammers, tools, tool boxes, drill bit sets... on and on.... for
like $45 bucks.. JACKPOT.

The GREAT thing is, a lot of the tools I bought that day I'd been scoping
out and looking for at Home Depot and Lowe's over the entire year and
didn't want to cough up like $35 for a stupid hammer or $85 for a wheel
barrow. But garage sales are a JACKPOT.

Craigslist and pawn shops are huge too man. I actually found my Stihl
badass chainsaw at a garage sale for $40 bucks.. lol

Man that's a $350 chainsaw. All my backpack blowers Craigslist.
Walk-behinds, push-mowers....everything. Whatever you do. Don't be
tempted EVEN IF you have the money to spare. Don't buy new
equipment until you can easily and absolutely afford to.

Being in business comes with constant and never ending expensive
surprises and the last thing you can afford in business is to be caught
broke. Heed my warnings.

WORK WITH WHAT YOU HAVE

This one is a huge point. Working with what you have, instead of going out
and buying the upgraded piece of equipment is also the secret that helped
me get from zero to $100,000 Fast.

See, let's say you only have a walk-behind... but you're starting to get these

big huge lawn accounts. You find yourself going on Craigslist and the
local equipment dealer constantly and obsessing over a new or used riding
mower. You keep repeating to yourself.
"Man...if I only just bought the rider right now, I'd fly through those lawns so
much faster"...

Well, You see where I'm going with this. Unless you're so swamped with
large accounts and have a large amount of money in the bank to easily buy
a rider....then

IT'S JUST YOUR EGO PLAYING HEAD GAMES WITH YOU!!!

Run that Walk-behind until either your wheels, or your legs fall off.
TRUST ME dammit. unless you have the work, cash-flow and winter work
and hella money saved up. Work with what you have and buy used shit
slowly and consistently. I have this golden rule and it's worked wonders for
my business.

I never ever buy a piece of equipment until I absolutely need it.
What I mean is... I don't buy the damn piece of equipment that I need
until the JOB IS SOLD, the PAPERWORK is signed and I'm literally ON
THE WAY to do the clients job.
That way your hard-earned money is being put to use for a return on your
investment immediately. BINGO BANGO!

Chapter 18

ABOUT PRICING

Pricing is all different depending on where you're at in your business. This
can be very simple and very complex at the same time my friend. What one
business owner gives you advice on will completely contradict what another
business owner tells you... on and on until infinity.

IT REALLY DEPENDS ON WHERE YOU'RE AT IN YOUR BUSINESS

When you first get started, hey.. you gotta make money and you may not
be aware or

EVEN CAPABLE OF UNDERSTANDING OVERHEAD COSTS.

I'm talking about all of the serious and critical overhead costs that come
into play when quoting, pricing and estimating landscape and lawn jobs.
I almost don't even know where to start here and
I don't want to lead you in the wrong direction but here's some basic
numbers to go off of.

DISCLAIMER: If I told you to charge $45 per man hr. and $135 an hour

for a 3 man crew. Because of insurance, payroll, taxes, overhead,
fuel, equipment, markup, labor, workmans compensation etc. That advice would probably do you NO GOOD WHATSOEVER
if your brand new and JUST getting started.
But If I told you to shoot for $35 an hour just for yourself while working "ON

THE JOB" as a place to start. "WHEN QUOTING" That'll make a little more
sense.... for now.

In all honestly, my first year in business I only averaged $10 an hour profit.
2nd year was $12-15 ... then leveled out at $17 an hr for a year.

Then Finally learned more about business and leveled out at $20 an hr.

NOTE: These numbers might seem very low.

I'm talking about profit for every hour worked including, driving in between
jobs, talking on the phone, doing paperwork at night and quoting jobs on

Sundays.

These numbers also are averaged out across the entire year INCLUDING 4
months of winter.

"Some weeks you'll make $10,000 a week, Some weeks you'll make
ZERO.
So, unless you buy my video training courses and watch my YouTube
channel, I can't really give your more advice about pricing rather than.
"Shoot for NO LESS Than $35 an hour " for yourself.

Translated, that means. "If based on experience, you think it will take 10
hrs to do a job, then charge $350" Simple as pie.
After all expenses and a 30%-50% profit margin, you should come out
making $15 an hr. profit.
"$15 an hr???? WHAT BITCH...THAT'S PEANUTS!!!"

Well...

As you learn the ropes of business and time goes on.
You'll raise your prices more and more...and more and more.

The biggest thing I can say is that learning how to quote comes with time,
experience and picking the brains of other contractors.
Here's a cool tip: Go buy a stopwatch or basic swimmers watch from
Walmart for like $12 bucks and use the timer function to start clocking how
long it takes to knock out certain areas and projects.

OR LOOK AT YOUR WATCH AT LEAST EVERY 15 MINUTES.

This will begin to train your brain how long things take. Whether it's 1 man,
2 men, 3,4,5,6,7,8. You Start to get a 6th sense of how much to charge per

hour.
I literally walk around a property and blocks out sections and zones based
on time allotments and how long "HOW MANY HOURS" things will take to
complete.

Always round up and always charge the same hourly rates for drivetime
when transporting materials.
The price can rack up quick and you might feel like the customer will be
offended at your price and that might be true. But when the time comes in
the future when you're working 100 hours a week including Sundays to make
up for the money you didn't make all week, You'll learn. On a more

positive note. This is your company, this is your time to shine. You're the
BOSSMAN, You're the skilled entrepreneur who's orchestrating this whole

damn circus act, you're the one putting your balls on the line and
YOU'RE THE ONE WHO DESERVES TO GET PAID.
SO GO OUT THERE AND DO YOUR THING AND GET PAID.
OVER AND OVER AND OVER MY FRIEND.

IT'S TIME TO BE GREAT!
Congratulations...

Go out, tear it up and make some noise my friend.
I totally believe in you. You GOT THIS MAN!

p.s. In my next book we'll be going further in depth
about pricing, collecting money, taxes and all the infinite
variables that
come with owning a Lawn and Landscape business.

Thank you,

Keith Kalfas

The Landscaping Employee Trap

Special Thanks and Acknowledgements

In no particular order

Scotty Rais

Many thanks for the continued Golden Nuggets of wisdom to my Great

friend Scotty Rais, CO-FOUNDER of "Maiden Detroit" Digital Media.

I don't know where I'd be without you bro

Dan Ivers

CO-FOUNDER of "Maiden Detroit" Digital Media.

Man your a wealth of unlimited cut and dry knowledge when it comes to

being a great friend and a genius at multimedia, design, videography etc.

on and on.. you've not only taught me so much, but made me laugh my ass

off in the process.

Anthony Vitale

President of "The Wealth System Inc."

Dude, if it weren't for you. The Landscaping Employee Trap wouldn't even

exist. I remember you telling me to start a youtube channel on how to start

a landscaping company. You saw the future, as usual.

Matt Brown

Bro, I remember on my wedding I was freaking out and hoping everything

was going smooth and you took me to the side and told me to chill out and

enjoy myself. Great friend

Coach Rob

Bro, if it weren't for you I'd be a wuss in a nuthouse by now. Thank you for

your wisdom and guidance www.EgoEdge.com

Al Czarniak

Thanks for being a center of balance in my life and coming up with all these

great ideas my friend.

Greg Chism

Man You've coached me through some rough spots when I didn't

understand why all these people were hating on me. haha

It's all just part of the game son.

Stan Genadek

Man you've taken the time out behind the scenes to coach me through

rough patches and your belief in God shines through your integrity. Thank

you.

Eric Reno

Like comrades we came from the same shit and both turned out alright.

Thanks for having my back all these years.

Jeff Allan

Not only a mentor, but a future vision of myself. You've been a damn good

coach to me man.

William Elling

I've called you up when I wanted nothing more than to die and you've stood by my side like a brother from another mother. Also took the time to teach

me shit no one else would have ever cared to.

Andrew Sonntag

The most level-headed genius I know. Every word that comes from your

mouth is the most positive millionaire-inspiring shit I've ever heard. Thank

you.

SPECIAL THANKS to MY FRIENDS ACROSS THE COUNTRY

Geek To Freak

Randy Mikhaiel

Top Notch Lawn Care

B&B Lawn Care

Johnny Mow

Nick Johnson

JC's Lawn Tips

Zack's Lawn Care

Greg's Mowing

A&S LawnScapes

SEF The Lawn Surgeon

Meebs Mowing Lawn Service

Triple-D's Lawn Care

Mowguy Fudd

K33MO

B&M Lawn Care

Jon Zimmerman

Wombat Gardens

JG Lawncare

Kendell Pro Services

Gerald Henry

Small Business & Fitness

Zeffer Lawn Care

Jordan Garcia

Mostly Humble 1

Shannon Cornthwaite

Lawn Care Rookie

Felix Blanco

EuroYard

JSTU 45

Brite Green Lawn Care

Marcos Carmona

Matt's Lawn Care & Graphics

Guns & Knives

Phil DiMonte

Chris Davies

Catlin Foster

Juan Perez

Erik Del Real

Brandon Herrman

Lawn Care Junkie

Kendrick Thomas

Moe's Lawn Care

CJ Storms

Matthew Thurmond

Lawn Care Bryan

Don Abraham

Nenad Mrakovic

Empire Lawns

Paul Bali

Sa Mowing Lawn Care

Prs22Sg

Primo Landscaping

James Villegas

Tanasi Time

Michigan Mowing

Alex Matthews

John Ryan

Mow Lawn Care

Taylor Sanchez

Collin Simpson

K and R Lifestyle

Jose Villagomez

I mentioned my top subscribers

If I didn't mention you "Nothing Personal" I can't type thousands of names

or I'm just plain tired because I stayed up until 4am for weeks on end

finishing this book.. haha. Love you fools Peace Out – Let's Get Our Dreams..

How to Start a Landscaping Business

RIGHT NOW! With NO Startup Money

(Copyright 2016)

GreenWorld Publishing

The Landscaping Employee Trap

Author,

Entrepreneur,

YouTube Personality

Keith Kalfas

Founder,

The Landscaping Employee Trap

www.TheLandscapingEmployeeTrap.com

P.S Find The AudioBook Version and Video Training Course on my

Website www.TheLandscapingEmployeeTrap.com

If You Like This, Then Check Out My Entire How To Start a Landscaping

Business Training Series on Audible, Amazon Kindle, and My Website

Mp3, Video, Audiobook, Directly to your laptop or Smartphone.

www.TheLandscapingEmployeeTrap.com

Disclaimer: This book is less about the modalities and methods about on how to actually perform And install professional landscapes and more about how to overcome the inner conflict and self-doubt that stops most first-time small business owners from leaving their dead-end jobs and starting their own small businesses. It's true that starting a landscaping business is incredibly challenging and time-consuming. It's true that I replaced my income from my job and only 6 weeks. I cannot promise you the same results. The tips and advice in this book are only my opinion and are not the opinions of critically acclaimed Landscaping organizations. The advice in this book shall be deemed for entertainment purposes only and is subject to change with time. The opinions in this book are only based on my story from personal experience. Do not take my advice and opinions as absolute fact. Do your own research and come to your own conclusions to find what works best for you. Also, before starting a small business. seek consultation from a professional CPA or accountant in your state or province who specializes in setting up tax structures and licensing for small businesses. Also consult with an insurance agent to get the proper insurances in place before performing work on anyone else's property but your own. Always be safe and practice safety. Good luck on your new small business.

Made in the USA
Middletown, DE
24 February 2023